It's All about the

Chirp, Snap, and Quack

By

Nancy M. Rollins

Copyright @ Nancy M. Rollins, 2016
ISBN-13: 978-1523283620
ISBN-10: 1523283629
Library of Congress Control Number: 2016900638
CreateSpace Independent Publishing Platform, North Charleston, SC
Photos used as illustrations are the property of the author, Nancy M. Rollins
Book cover, formatting and book interior design www.goldenboxbooks.com

Happy people share a smile.

I quack!

It's all in the step.

Don't stand too close!

A gator's lunch may be over in a snap.

Awww!

Finally reached that itch.

Trying to hide.

Perhaps those pesky females won't spot me here.

DELICIOUS!

When it comes to nuts,
I can never have enough.

Many problems could be solved

with one soft peck.

Okay Helen,

next time you should pick the place.

Best friends are made

One quack at a time.

Grumpy or lonely,

show them love every day.

One of us is clearly

an impostor.

What can I say?

She likes my quack.

Saturday Morning Clean Up.

Deposit all edible garbage swiftly into the belly.

Easter drop.

What manner of shenanigans is this?

Home can be any place

that makes you happy.

Buddies often quibble

especially, when the male ducks outnumber the females by two.

Fess up!

Did you eat my treat?

Oh, Pl-e-a-s-e!
Turtles don't move slowly.

They just prefer not to rush through life.

Hungry little ducky goes

quack, quack, quack.
What yummy morsel has she
found?

It's the simple pleasures I need,

but a fish would be so nice!

I'm not sharing!

Young love can make

an inseparable pair.

After a busy day

even a squirrel needs a nap
Zzzzzzzz!

Moments are remembered fondly

when shared with a friend.

When society stops listening,

voices are merely squawks and squeals.

Motherhood is

the joy of life.

Maintaining a watchful eye.

Is misfortune near?

A long snout is

ready to snap at whatever moves.
Ouch!

This hawk is about to eat.

Care to share a fresh kill?

A bird's peaceful song.

Chirp! Chirp!
Will a future mate hear her call?

Determination.

Small imperfections do not lessen the spirit within.

This is my intimidating look.

Aren't you scared?

Didn't Mom ever tell you that

ignoring someone is impolite?

A welcome beam of sunshine

helps brighten up the day.

Don't leave!

Let's quack and make up.

We can never have enough

friends in our lives.

Cheer up folks!

Everyone has a bad day to appreciate the ones that are good.

When choosing a new leader,

let personal integrity decide.

You may outrun me

but I can be home in an instant.

I don't believe it!

Fleas again!

Rest period is over!

Forward, march!

Food fight!

Swallowing quickly ensures a treat.

How did I end up here?

Does anyone have an escape plan?

Now this is an awkward moment,

caught between p–u–s–h and unexpected guests.

A world without diversity

is sluggishly dull.

Enjoying a bird's eye view of the water,

diving for fish is a solo act.

If wildlife can live in harmony,

✕✕✕

✕✕✕

why can't we?

Hee-hee-hee! I'm a fake alligator.

Had you fooled!

Thank you for reading.

When visiting wildlife, always be kind.

The Author

www.authornancymrollins.blogspot.com

Formally a resident of New Hampshire, a move relocates Nancy to the warm Florida coast. Here, with her family, she finds herself delightfully, a grandmother of four. With hobbies of writing, graphic designs, and photography, her goal is to turn them into a lasting career.

Florida is known for its frequent sunshine and tourism. Sometimes, even the most common park locations attract visitors to their natural, wildlife environments. Birds, ducks, and squirrels often venture near humans, hoping for crumbs of food. In such locations, even the most amateur photographer could easily capture the daily activities of these extraordinary creatures.

Nancy keeps her camera close, but also a pencil and notebook too. She believes each photo has a voice eager to be expressed. Dramatizing a natural occurrence within the photos, she combines humorous phases and fictional, wildlife fun. All About the Chirp, Snap and Quack is an entertaining exhibit for animal lovers everywhere.

www.ingramcontent.com/pod-product-compliance
Lightning Source LLC
Chambersburg PA
CBHW041512280526
45792CB00004B/1226